PIANO · VOCAL · GUITAR

WHERE I FIND YOU

2   STEADY MY HEART

7   WE ARE

16   ONE DESIRE

24   FIND YOU ON MY KNEES

32   SAVIOR'S HERE

44   STARS IN THE SKY

52   WHAT LOVE IS THIS

60   RUN TO YOU (I NEED YOU)

69   RISE

76   LOVE CAME DOWN

85   WE EXALT YOUR NAME

94   HERE

ISBN 978-1-4584-2145-6

7777 W. BLUEMOUND RD. P.O. BOX 13819 MILWAUKEE, WI 53213

Visit Hal Leonard Online at
www.halleonard.com

Steady My Heart

Words and Music by MATT BRONLEEWE,
KARI JOBE and BEN GLOVER

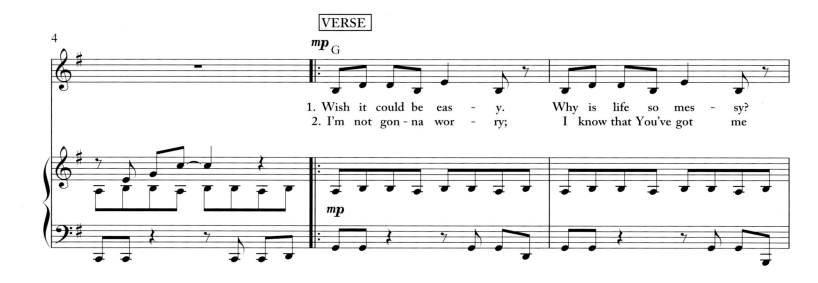

6

CODA

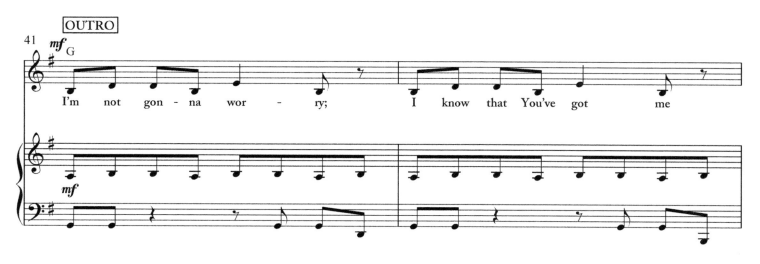

OUTRO

I'm not gon - na wor - ry; I know that You've got me

right in - side the palm of Your hand. _____

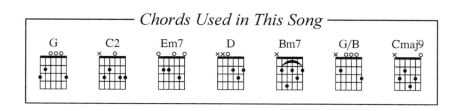

Chords Used in This Song

G   C2   Em7   D   Bm7   G/B   Cmaj9

We Are

Words and Music by CHUCK BUTLER,
ED CASH, JAMES TEALY
and HILLARY McBRIDE

VERSE 2

2. We are called ___ to spread ___ the news, ___ to tell the world ___ ___ the sim - ple truth. ___ Je - sus came ___ ___ to ___ save, ___ there's free - dom in ___ His name, ___

Lyrics:

91 We are the light of the world, and we got-ta, we got-ta, we got-

94 -ta let the light shine. We are the light of the world,

97 we are the cit-y on a hill. We are the

100 light of the world, and we got-ta, we got-ta, we got-ta let the light shine.

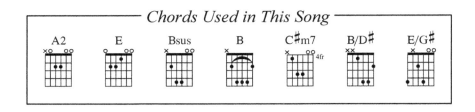

One Desire

Words and Music by JASON INGRAM
and KARI JOBE

My heart will al-ways sing I love You, I love You. My

heart will al - ways sing I love You, I love You. My

heart will al - ways sing I love You.

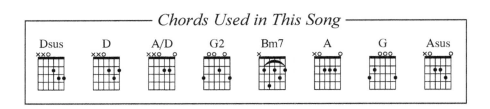

Chords Used in This Song

Find You on My Knees

Words and Music by MATT BRONLEEWE,
KARI JOBE and BEN GLOVER

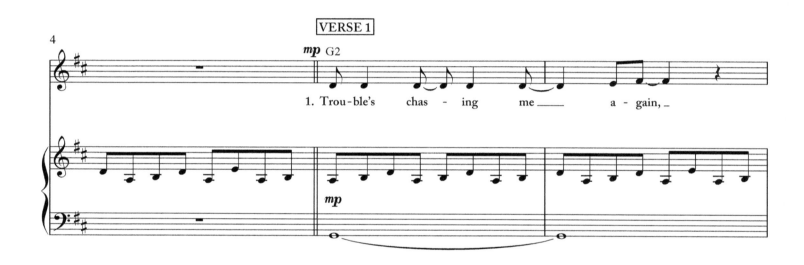

26

82 Bm7 A
leave me thirst - y. _____ When I am

85 Em7 Bm7 A
weak, when I am lost and search - ing, _____ I

88 G2
find You on ___ my ___ knees. _____

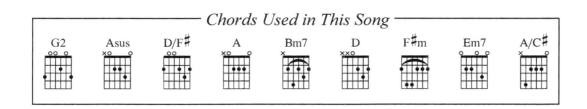

Chords Used in This Song

G2   Asus   D/F#   A   Bm7   D   F#m   Em7   A/C#

Savior's Here

Words and Music by KARI JOBE
and CODY CARNES

Capo 1 (G)

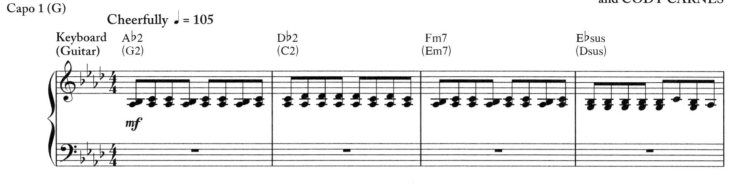

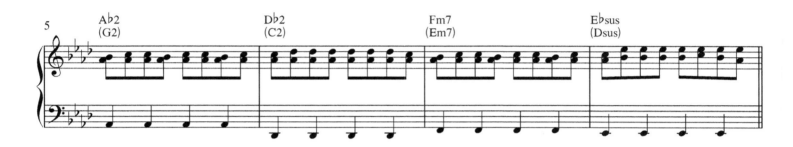

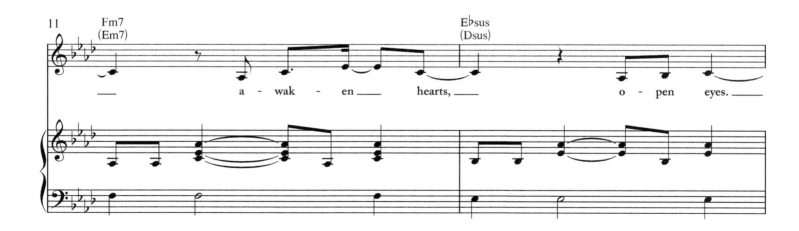

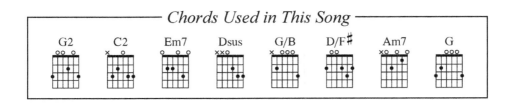

Stars in the Sky

Words and Music by KARI JOBE
and CHRIS AUGUST

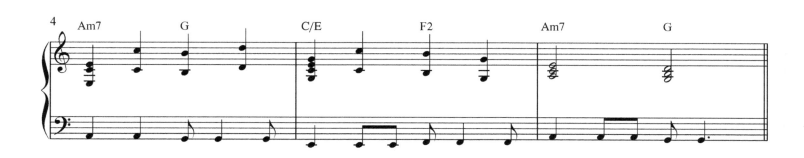

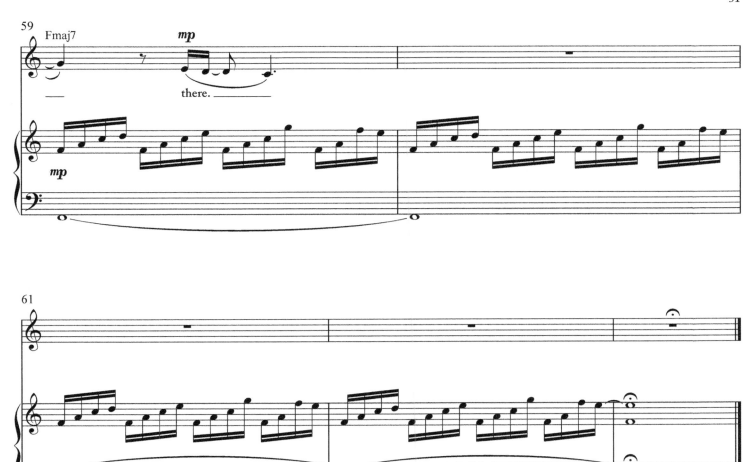

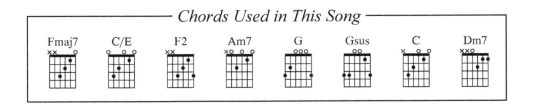

What Love Is This

Words and Music by KARI JOBE,
LINCOLN BREWSTER and MIA FIELDES

-ow of ___ the cross, I'm o - ver - whelmed ___ that I keep find-

CHORUS

-ing o - pen arms. ___ What love ___ is this, ___ that ___ You gave ___

___ Your ___ life ___ for me, ___ and made ___ a way ___

___ for me ___ to know ___ You? And I ___ con - fess, ___ You're

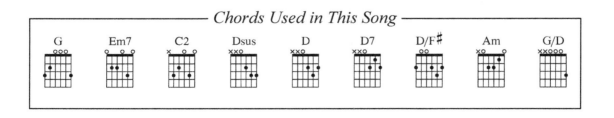

Chords Used in This Song

Run to You
(I Need You)

Words and Music by KARI JOBE,
ED CASH, MATT BURROWES, TIM PETERS,
JANELL BELCHER, JASON BELCHER
and JORDAN MACKENZIE

Capo 2 (E)

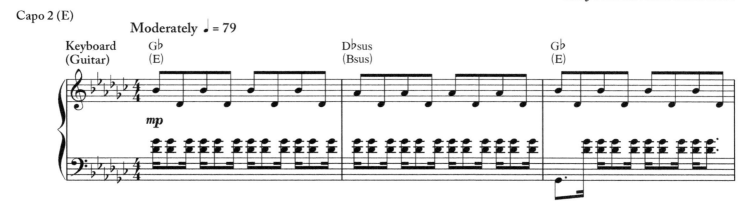

VERSE 1

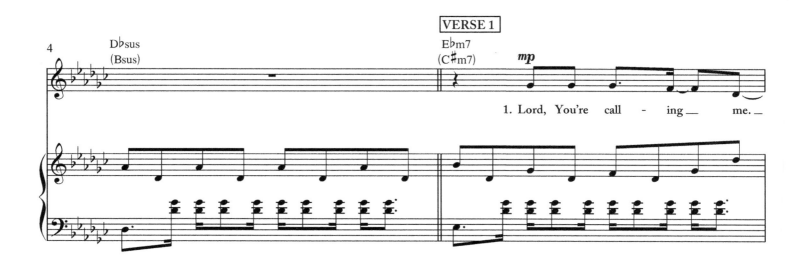

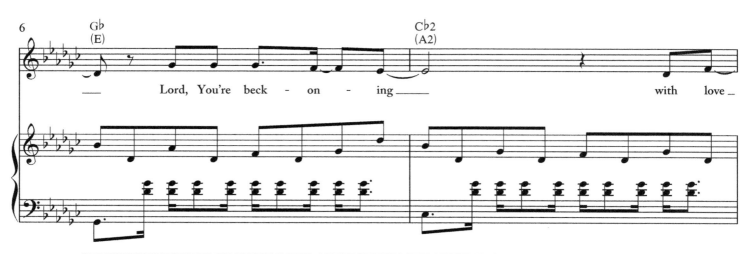

64

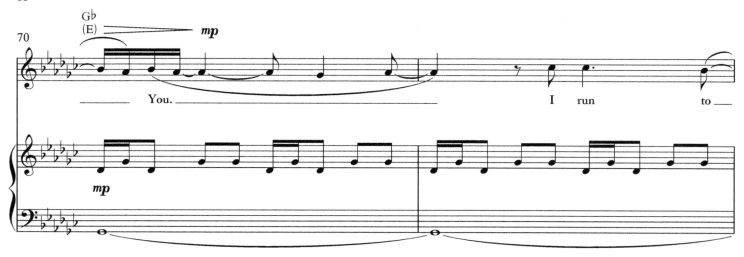

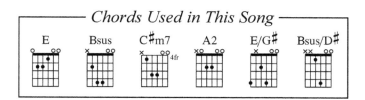

Rise

Words and Music by MATT BRONLEEWE
and KARI JOBE

Moderately ♩ = 93

VERSE

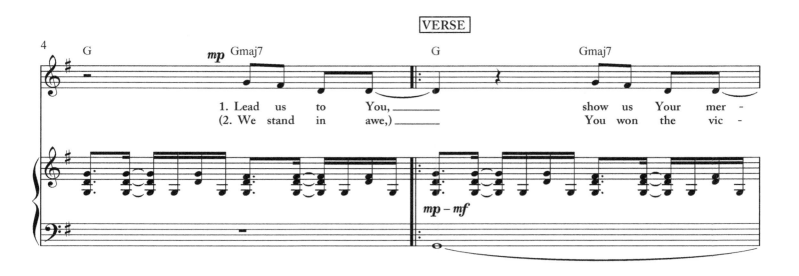

1. Lead us to You, _____ show us Your mer-
(2. We stand in awe,) _____ You won the vic-

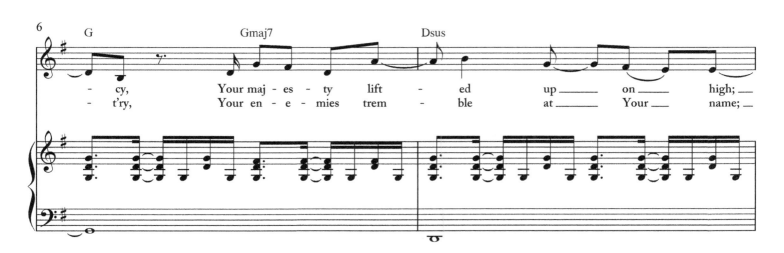

-cy, Your maj - es - ty lift - ed up _____ on _____ high; _____
-t'ry, Your en - e - mies trem - ble at _____ Your _____ name; _____

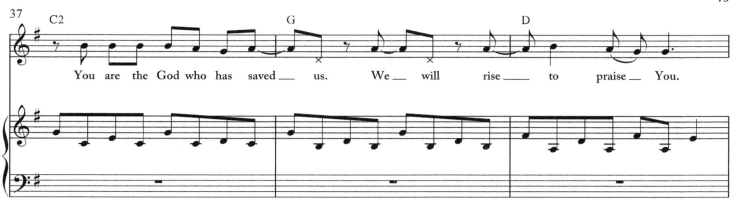

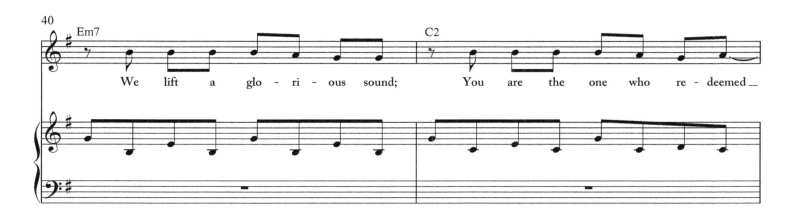

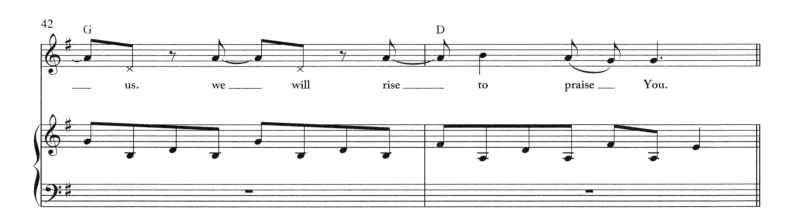

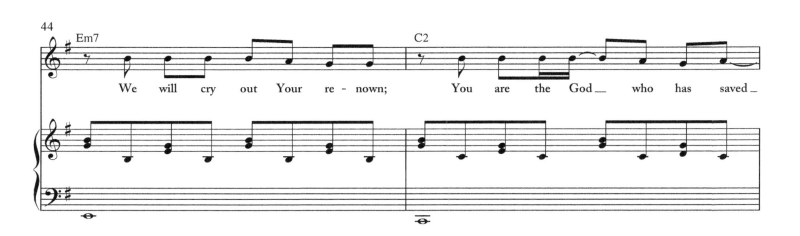

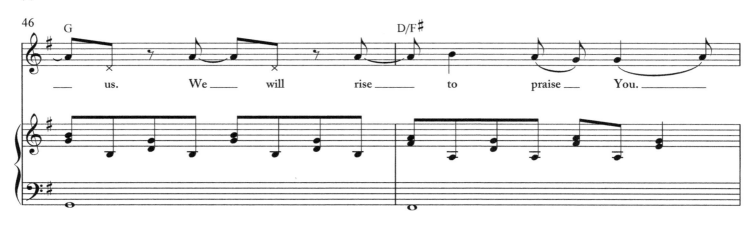

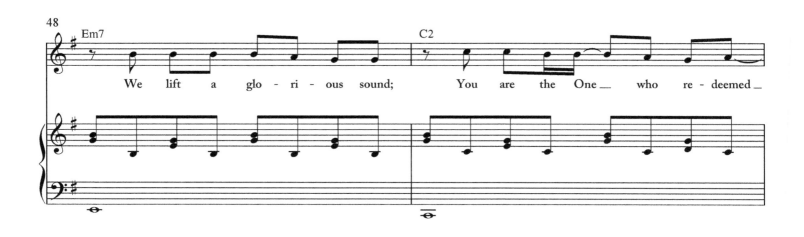

rise. _____ Yeah yeah yeah yeah yeah. __

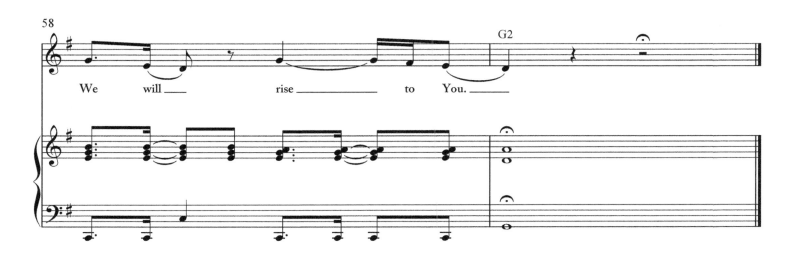

We will ____ rise _____ to You. _____

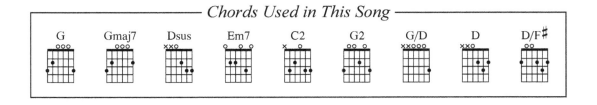

Chords Used in This Song

Love Came Down

Words and Music by JEREMY RIDDLE,
JEREMY EDWARDSON, IAN McINTOSH
and BRIAN JOHNSON

Capo 1 (G)

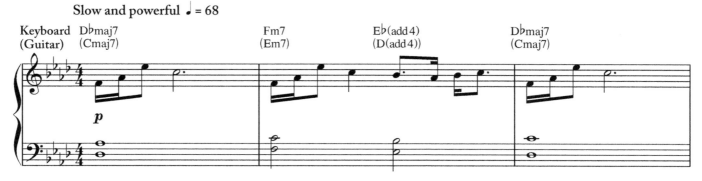

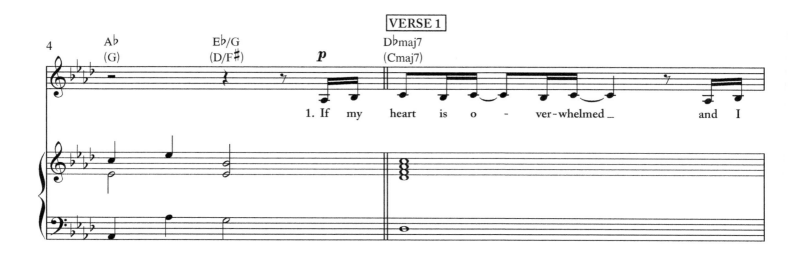

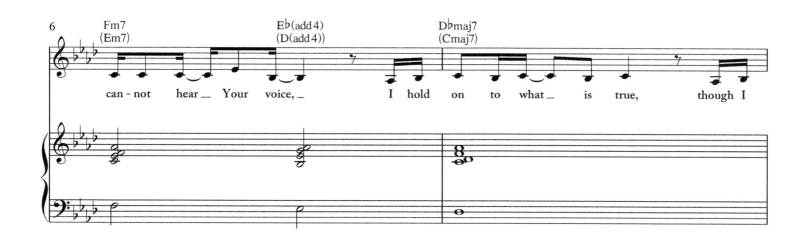

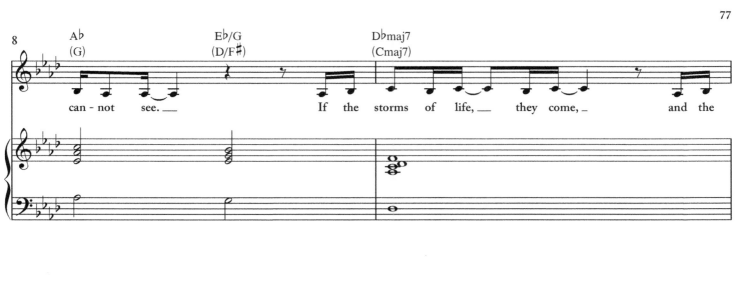

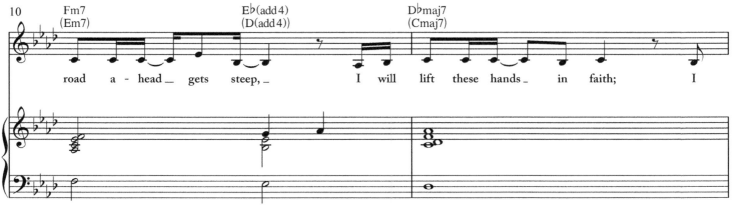

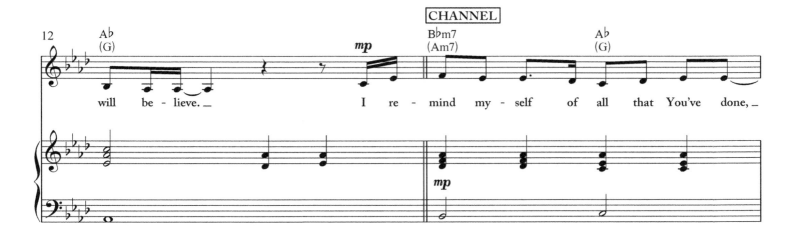

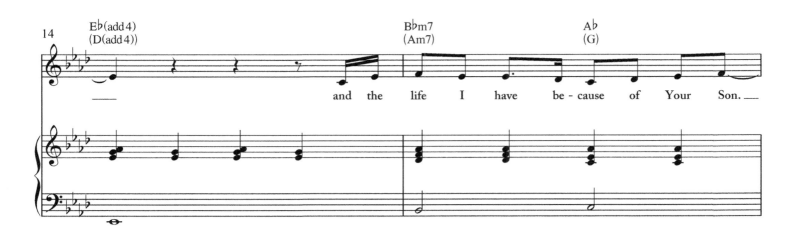

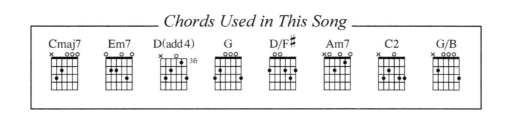

We Exalt Your Name

Words and Music by KARI JOBE
and MATT MAHER

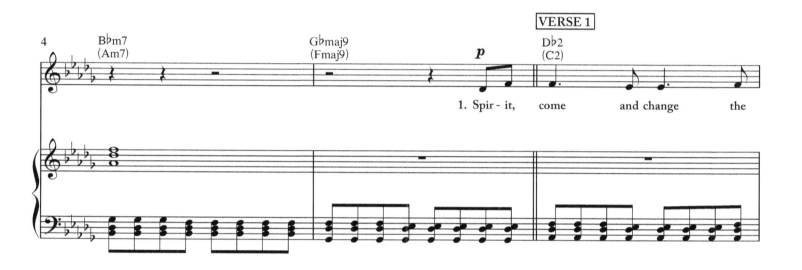

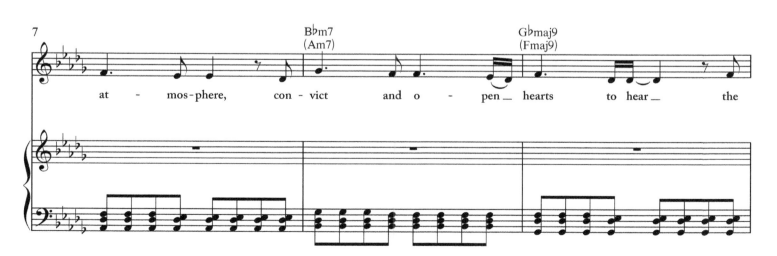

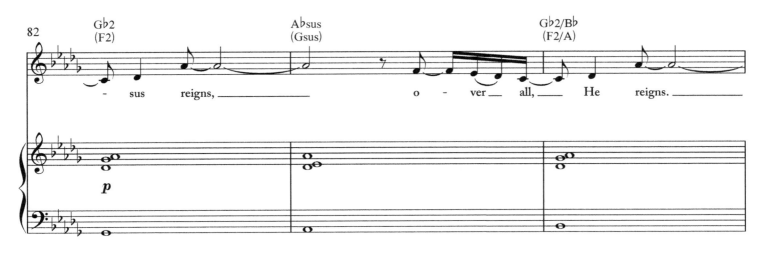

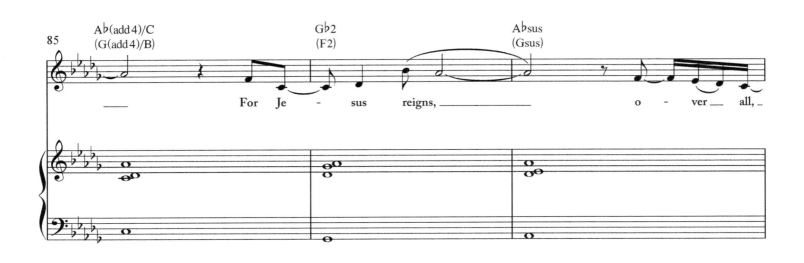

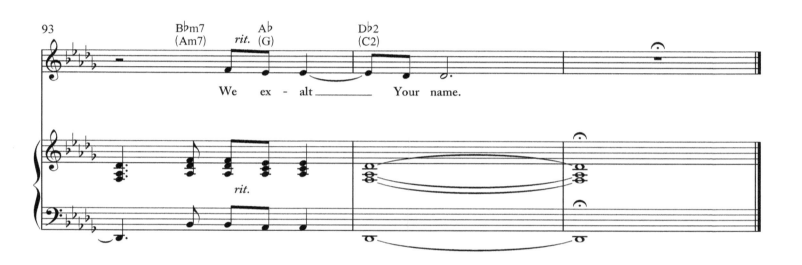

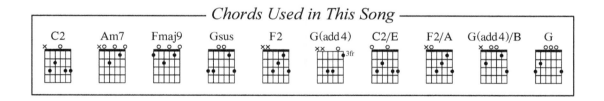

Here

Words and Music by KARI JOBE,
DAVID LEONARD and LESLIE JORDAN

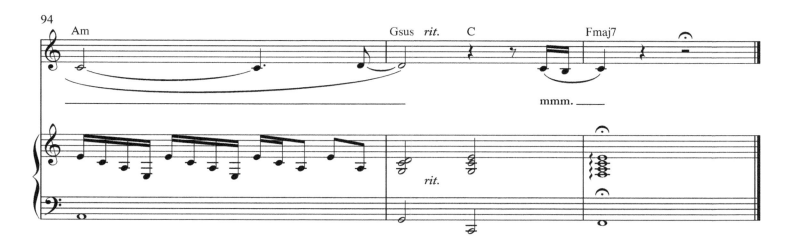

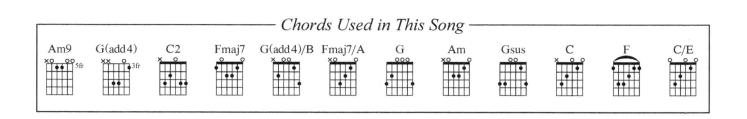